# Dating Tips for Men

## 11 Dating Tips and Dating Advice for Men to Get a Girlfriend and Keep Her

by Michelle Winters

# Table of Contents

Introduction ................................................................ 1

Dating Tip #1: Know Who You Are! ........................... 7

Dating Tip #2: Get to Work on The Negative List
............................................................................... 13

Dating Tip #3: Understanding and Boosting
Confidence .............................................................. 17

Dating Tip #4: Grooming Yourself for Success ....... 23

Dating Tip #5: Be Proactive Not Reactive ................ 25

Dating Tip #6: Never Be a Tool ................................. 29

Dating Tip #7: Stay Faithful to Your Tastes ............. 33

Dating Tip #8: But Don't Let Them Define You ..... 35

Dating Tip #9: Be Chivalrous, Not Sexist ................. 39

Dating Tip #10: Always Be Prepared ........................ 43

Dating Tip #11: Listen and Share, But Don't
Overwhelm .............................................................. 47

Conclusion ................................................................ 49

# Introduction

So, you've been to every dating site and back, tried every theory and shenanigan mentioned in books and articles, watched every movie on the matter, yet you're no closer to cracking the code to the complexities of dating.

Well, maybe this will cheer you up. Most girls are just as confused about it as you are. There are more rules and games today in interpersonal relationships than ever and no overall guide. They're all over the place and it's hard to know which to follow.

But, what if there was an easier way out? What if there was a way to short-circuit the games altogether? I'm going to tell you a way to step around the whole 'twenty mind-games between each milestone' BS that's becomes the face of most dating scenarios today.

Well, in case you haven't fully understood yet, there is one way - Stop Playing The Game. Now, I can practically *hear* most of you saying something to the tune of, "Yeah, right," or "Easier said than done." But, there's a simple set of rules to follow with which you can stop playing the game on the terms of others, and even position the odds in your favor. And so, I present to you this short-read book.

Prepare yourself to learn everything you need to know about getting your dream girl, and keeping her interested in you. Are you ready to shrug off a lifetime of bad dating experiences and finally take the first steps into the life you *know* you deserve? Well then, let's get started!

© Copyright 2014 by LCPublifish LLC - All rights reserved.

This document is geared towards providing reliable information in regard to the topic and issue covered. The publication is sold with the idea that the publisher is not required to render accounting, officially permitted, or otherwise, qualified services. If advice is necessary, legal or professional, a practiced individual in the profession should be ordered.

- From a Declaration of Principles which was accepted and approved equally by a Committee of the American Bar Association and a Committee of Publishers and Associations.

In no way is it legal to reproduce, duplicate, or transmit any part of this document in either electronic means or in printed format. Recording of this publication is strictly prohibited and any storage of this document is not allowed unless with written permission from the publisher. All rights reserved.

The information provided herein is stated to be truthful and consistent, in that any liability, in terms of inattention or otherwise, by any usage or abuse of any policies, processes, or directions contained within is solely and completely the responsibility of the recipient reader. Under no circumstances will any legal responsibility or blame be held against the publisher for any reparation, damages, or monetary loss due to the information herein, either directly or indirectly.

Respective authors own all copyrights not held by the publisher.

The information herein is offered for informational purposes solely, and is universal as so. The presentation of the information is without contract or any type of guarantee assurance.

The trademarks that are used are without any consent, and the publication of the trademark is without permission or backing by the trademark owner. All trademarks and brands within this book are for clarifying purposes only and are the owned by the owners themselves, not affiliated with this document.

# Dating Tip #1: Know Who You Are!

If you don't want to end up being everybody's puppet for the rest of your life, you need to understand your own strengths and weaknesses. The easiest people to lead around by the nose are those made to believe *they're* the ones *choosing* to follow.

Others can take advantage of you by playing up your strengths and giving you opportunities to hide your weaknesses – that is until your usefulness runs out.

In other words, people are able to exploit your nature only when you don't completely understand it yourself. Of course, everyone gets mad when the mean girl exploits the vulnerable geek guy in a movie. But, real life is not as clear-cut as the movies. When you don't have a firm grasp of your strengths and weaknesses - of who you are - it's hard to realize when the same situation happens to you. When someone is manipulating you like a puppet. You don't see when it happens to you because, like all humans, it's difficult to get a realistic perspective on something when you are in the middle of it. We tend to think that, even if a woman treated her last four boyfriends like her personal puppets, you're *different*, the exception – she won't treat you the same way. And you get into the foggy state of denial – not seeing things as they really are.

So, it's important to take some time and figure out who you are – your likes and dislikes, your character's strengths and flaws. There's an easy exercise that you can do to help with this. The catch is, you'll have to be extremely and brutally honest with yourself for it to actually work.

Take two sheets of paper, then write all your positive qualities on one sheet and all the negative ones on the other. Include **everything**. Positive examples could be - you love reading books, pursuing random tidbits of knowledge, speak multiple languages, you can hold your liquor, know how to dance decently, are chivalrous, have a good sense of humor, and so forth. Negative examples could be - you spend too much time on the computer, ignore your health, have low self-esteem, don't pay attention to your clothing, don't take care of your appearance, or you're insensitive sometimes, and so on. Again, it's important to be completely honest with yourself throughout the exercise. Even if something is hard to admit or accept, put it on the list. This list is for your eyes only, and is not meant to be shared with anyone else. Keep it in a private, secure place because this will most likely be the most personal thing you'll ever put on paper.

In your first attempt, write at least twenty positive and twenty negative qualities about yourself. If you can't seem to think of that many, then you're either not taking this exercise as seriously as you should and thus not as interested in taking control of your dating life as you claim, or you're not being completely honest. *Everyone* has at least twenty positive and negative qualities, if not many more. After all, we all have *at least* 40 things that make up our character and personality.

Once you've written twenty each, try to extend each list in equal quantities. If you add three more negatives, then add three more positives as well. Once you get past twenty-five on each, read through both lists. Read through each quality and accept it for what it is. Separate your ego and self-worth from this list, approaching it the same way you would an intellectual problem. Your sense of self-worth and personality is initially shaped by every experience in your life - what you've been taught from your environment, and how you've learned to deal with different scenarios. Your strength of *character* however, comes from how you take your experiences, what you were taught and self-knowledge, then put it to good use. Understand the difference?

If a knife-wielding serial killer's son grows up to be a serial killer as well and defends himself saying, "What choice did I have? That's what I learned from my dad", his character is very bad because he has a weak sense of himself. He hasn't tried to truly know himself and his motives – thus he hasn't tried to break away from the pattern learned from his father. Now, if that same guy grew up to be an excellent surgeon who saved hundreds of lives, he would have an incredibly good and strong character. You can only use your own strengths and weaknesses to the advantage of yourself and others if you *know* them to begin with.

# Dating Tip #2: Get to Work on The Negative List

I'm sure that out of all those negative qualities, more than half of them can be easily resolved now that you've identified them. For example, if you have a habit of saying the wrong thing at the wrong time, spend the next three days talking less and concentrating more on listening. For every three things that you want to say in a conversation, allow yourself to say only one of them out loud. If you tend to be a little too quiet, then push yourself to say at least three things in every conversation you're a part of. If you think you don't read enough books, pick up one in a genre that interests you. Get the picture?

The objective is to change at least a few of the negative qualities into positive ones by the end of each week. Identifying and accepting your problem traits is only the first step. Now you have to take action and use that knowledge to convert them into traits to add onto your 'positive' list. If you're having trouble in your dating life, it could be one of many issues. Perhaps you're interesting enough, but too shy and plagued with self-esteem or trust issues to let others get to know you. On the other hand, you might not come off as an interesting person, failing to portray yourself in a positive light, so others can't see just how interesting you are. Sometimes you might just be trying way too hard to impress and come off as 'fake' or simply not showing your true self to a date. Trying too hard also can come off as 'full of yourself' even if that's not the impression you meant.

No matter which one of these issues hinders your dating experience, creating the two lists and working on the negative ones will help solve them. If you've ever been attracted to someone, think about which qualities, besides the physical ones, attracted you to them. Do you have as many attractive qualities to draw others to you as well? If the answer is 'no' or you're not sure, then maybe work on picking up a few more skills and talents to boost your appeal. Try your hand at sketching, download music mixers, learn to skateboard; pick up the guitar, take a cooking class (women love a guy who can cook), and so on. The possible avenues for self-improvement are endless, and it could be fun in the process.

On the other hand, if you do have a long list of attractive skills and qualities but still have trouble in the dating arena, you'll need to figure out what else could be holding you back.

# Dating Tip #3: Understanding and Boosting Confidence

To succeed in the world of dating, you need to first understand the basics of how attraction works. Contrary to what most people think, physical characteristics like your height, facial features and the shape of your body only play a small part of it all. The fundamentals of attractions are based in **body language**.

While people who have attractive physical traits are more pleasing to the eye, it's the *confidence* that they get from having those qualities that makes all the difference. As a friend of mine puts it, good looks only help in those few moments it takes a woman to walk from where she stands to where you are. Beyond that, if you open your mouth and end up a total dunce, you'll turn any quality woman off faster than you can say your name. So, even if you don't have the attractive physical traits you'd like, you can still ignite that initial attraction, the one that makes a woman walk up to you, by working on the right body language.

Basically, you need to send the impression that you're not just another 'Beta' but a strong and sturdy 'Alpha'. Again, this has nothing to do with physical strength. After all, the most powerful men in the world aren't the ones who spend their days wrestling on a canvas mat. Apart from the body language, it's the mind that separates an effective leader from their followers.

The easiest way to do this is to project confidence. Again, confidence doesn't mean being an obnoxious douchebag or having the slick charm of a typical player. Thankfully, confidence is definitely one of those things that's easy to 'fake it till you make it'.

For starters, you need to work on the way you hold yourself and how you walk and talk. Always hold your head high and make solid eye contact with everyone. I understand that this may be difficult for some of you, but this is only the beginning – and it's worth it.

When you're walking, don't hunch your shoulders. Hold them back and slightly pressed down, powerful yet relaxed – you don't want to appear too stiff. Keep your back straight but relaxed at all times and stick your chest slightly out, even if you don't think you have much of one. Take mid to longish strides while you walk, and never hurry or run if you don't have to. Again, remember to keep your head high and always make eye contact. Don't be afraid of holding eye contact for a few seconds before you look away. Keep a slightly ironic smile on your face at most times, subtly turning one side of your mouth upwards. Let people wonder why you always have a mischievous smirk. It tends to put people slightly off their game if you look like you know something that you're not sharing with them. This is especially intriguing if a woman thinks the impish smile has to do with them.

When you speak, don't rush through words in a nervous tumble. Keep a lower or rougher tone of voice - I mean a deeper register of voice, not Batman or anything - when you're speaking about normal everyday things. And if you're standing, stand with your legs comfortably apart and in line with your shoulders.

But, understand the difference between confident and jerk-like. Don't make fun of others or crack inappropriate or mean jokes in an attempt to impress or make her laugh. No quality woman will think this is attractive. Instead, you'll come across as rude, insecure and about as intelligent as a Neanderthal.

Don't use curse words during any 'normal' conversation. It may seem strange and 'old-fashioned', but it works. You don't necessarily have to completely refrain from cursing, unless you want to. Just don't infuse cursing into every sentence – perhaps a mild one here and there. It's undignified and viewed as disrespectful by many women if you overdo it.

Now you have all the tricks to appearing confident. Repeat them often enough and they'll soon become habit. Whenever you feel like you need to boost that external confidence, pick up your positive qualities list and read it to yourself over and over again. *That's* how many things you bring to the table in any relationship, and any partner would be lucky to have you. Also, as you keep working on changing your negative qualities to positive ones, you'll feel a deep sense of satisfaction, achievement and, of course, confidence. As you move further along this path, you will get to a point where you won't even have to 'fake' confidence – it will come naturally and in abundance.

# Dating Tip #4: Grooming Yourself for Success

While this may not seem so important to you, it's **extremely** important to women. It doesn't matter to many quality women whether you look like James Bond or not, but it *does* matter to them that you take basic care of yourself.

So, always take some care of how you dress, your hygiene, and *always* make sure you smell good. However, don't float in a cloud of cologne – just a dab of some behind the ears or the base of your neck. Also put at least some thought into your hairstyle and fashion sense, especially around a woman you like.

This is all important because taking care of yourself sends the message "I like who I am, and so I take care of myself". If you don't like yourself enough to avoid walking around like a pig-sty, why should anyone else?

# Dating Tip #5: Be Proactive Not Reactive

If you have a girl you're attracted to, and you intend to be her 'man', then start acting like it. Take the courage to approach *her* and ask her out. Really, the worst that she can do is say no. I guarantee that the world will still go on spinning and you two will either hit it off or you'll move on to another girl. One who likes you back and deserves to be the recipient of all your love and attention.

Those are the only two scenarios, and neither of them end with the universe imploding. Stop waiting around for things to 'just go your way', or for the 'stars to align themselves'. The difference between dreamers and achievers is that achievers know when to stop dreaming and start making things happen.

Being reactive and waiting for your girl to drop into your lap is such an easily justifiable position. This position is filled with excuses that let you avoid facing the fact that you're wimping out. In the meanwhile, some slick playboy's going to walk in and sweep your girl off her feet while you make excuses like, "the time isn't right," and "well, now she's got a boyfriend and I can't possibly say anything *now*". Damn right you can't, but someone else got her first only because you never made your move.

And even if you think she couldn't *possibly* have said 'yes' either way, understand the basic point that no matter what you think of yourself, the chances of you getting her were **exactly 50%**. The difference between a 'yes' and a 'no'. Only two possible responses.

# Dating Tip #6: Never Be a Tool

No matter how much you try to improve yourself, you'll never progress if you devote your all in exchange for someone else's bare minimum. Turn it around - you wouldn't really be interested in a girl who gave you her all in exchange for the barest amount of effort from you. Would she make you want to try harder or be better for her sake? Probably not since it's hard to respect someone who's willing to be content with such little effort.

So, set up some boundaries and *stick to them*! Don't drop everything you're doing and rush over to someone else's side to chat about every little emotion or problem they have. You need to get over the 'knight in shining armor' syndrome. The quickest way to get friend-zoned is by being a handy 'tool' for someone else's troubles.

So, if you've set time apart for yourself, your friends or your interests – you *can* answer calls from the girl you like, but keep it short and make it clear that it's *your* time. Then go right back to what you were doing. Of course, you can help if there's a real emergency.

The message here is that if you don't respect your own needs and boundaries enough to take them into account, then why should anyone else respect them? Yes, plenty of guys are hopeless romantics who love to give their women everything they could possibly want. Yet, you need to find a way of doing it without losing respect. And even then, only *after* you've got them. After all, if you'd treat your girlfriend exactly like you'd treat a female friend you've got a crush on, what's the difference? There needs to be distinction between the two.

Even once you start dating, keep at least some time and space for your own hobbies and activities. And also give that same respect for time and space to your partner. The funny part here is that if you both have sedentary hobbies, you could have your own 'me' times while sitting in the same room as well. However, never neglect yourself entirely for the sake of another. Both of you will remain thankful that you did so a few years down the line.

# Dating Tip #7: Stay Faithful to Your Tastes

If you've already figured out your likes and dislikes by now, then remain faithful to them. Don't pander to someone else's opinion and agree with what they're saying, just because you're trying to connect with them. That's what 'people-pleasers' do, not equal partners. And no quality man or woman likes being with a sycophant.

Stay true to yourself, no matter how much risk you perceive in the possibility of a disagreement. Mature adults can handle disagreements calmly, with integrity, and with respect for other people's opinions.

# Dating Tip #8: But Don't Let Them Define You

However, this doesn't mean that you should close yourself off to new experiences. Remember one thing – always try something twice. This simple mantra will change your life. When people try something new the first time, expectations, misgivings, apprehension, etc. taints the experience – especially if you entered the experience believing you wouldn't enjoy it. But, if you try something twice, it gives you a solid, unbiased opinion. Always keep your mind open to new experiences, but make it clear that that's what you're doing. If you don't like something after you've tried it twice, make that clear.

An understanding woman doesn't need her partner to agree with everything she says, or to challenge everything she says and believes. It's not about agreeing or disagreeing all the time. It's about not letting your views to be swayed by the opinions of others. It makes you seem weak, indecisive and shaped by others around you rather than someone with a backbone of your own. True strength and confidence is about attempting everything that crosses your path without being bogged by narrow-mindedness or insecurities. But it also retains the integrity of character and voicing your true opinion.

You're not required to like everything your partner likes, but at least give everything a fair shot.

# Dating Tip #9: Be Chivalrous, Not Sexist

Most women love the attention of a chivalrous man. But chivalry doesn't mean that you're opening doors, pulling back chairs or offering your arm while walking because women *need* to be taken care of in some way. Chivalry, in modern times, means *knowing* that your lady is more than capable of taking care of herself, but you do it anyway as a way of showing your attention and affection.

Understand the difference? It means that if you're out with a girl that you like, keep your attention on her at all times. Take note of what she may like or need, and try to stay one step ahead of it. Of course, this doesn't apply to every waking moment of the day. But doing this on a date is a pleasant way of showing that you're interested enough to take care of the small things and make their time with you as pleasant as possible.

An obvious corollary to this is – if you're the one who proposed the first date, pick up the check. If your date insists otherwise beforehand, try to pick up the check anyway. But, if it seems that she continues to insist on paying, then be gracious enough to step back and let her. You don't want to come off as uncomfortably sexist or backward-thinking in such matters. Still, always offer nonetheless. And if you paid the check and she seems uncomfortable about it, be confident enough to say something like "How about you treat me to a cup of coffee tomorrow?". It'll suggest your confidence in getting a second date, and that you have no trouble accepting her paying for you, but you just wanted to pick up the check here since you're the one who suggested it.

# Dating Tip #10: Always Be Prepared

If you're asking a girl out on a date, always have the excursion planned ahead of time. While being spontaneous is fun, things can easily descend into a failed night with half-hearted attempts at impromptu plans that never quite pan out. Instead, prepare two to three different plans for one night, with two to three completely different sets of things to do.

Handle the reservations beforehand and get all necessary information, *then* you can decide which way to go at the spur of the moment. If the girl doesn't catch on to what you've done, she'll still enjoy the 'surprisingly' successful open-ended 'let's go where our mood takes us' feel to the night. And if she does catch on, well then, she'll be doubly impressed with the amount of effort you underwent to give her a fun night.

Don't project your likes and dislikes onto your date and plan accordingly. For the first date, choose neutral places that you both may enjoy and where you can get to know her better. And having planned multiple places, it'll pay off when you're prepping for the second date.

Once you start dating, keep up the preparatory streak. Always have a couple of back-up ideas ready so that what you actually end up doing once you step out is always left up to the mood of the night.

# Dating Tip #11: Listen and Share, But Don't Overwhelm

While a lot of women love having an interested ear to share their days and thoughts with, you need to be careful to let that develop slowly. When getting into a new dating experience with a guy, most women dislike having to 'tell everything' just yet. They want to share, gossip, laugh and chat – have a light, fun time. Many of them also want to hold their cards closely and seem mysterious until they're ready to share every detail with you.

So, especially when dating someone new, it's good to show an interest in the other person. But don't go overboard or let it develop into a one-sided conversation. Be prepared to share a bit of yourself as well, but don't choose stories or facts that evoke sympathy or pity. "Awwww," isn't really the strongest foundation on which to build a relationship.

# Conclusion

Stepping away from all the typical, complicated 'dating games' of today is easier than it may appear. As long as you make sure to protect your own interests against mind-games, you can develop a straightforward dating 'strategy' that will give you unprecedented success.

Don't over-share - too fast too soon. While it's certain that any quality woman likes knowing their partner intimately, they also like 'working' for it.

Don't be a 'nice guy' all the time. While they're kind and sweet and, well, nice – they evoke as much heat and passion as an ice-cube. But that doesn't mean you should act like a jerk either. Women enjoy the company of a 'bad boy' from time to time, and there's nothing wrong with being witty and 'wickedly' flirty – but know where to draw the line. Be nice from time to time and try to leave them guessing as to what you really are on the inside. Make them 'work' for the honor of knowing the 'real you'.

Don't lie. No matter how well you cover your tracks, it'll always come back to bite you. If it's important enough to lie for, then it's important enough for your girl to know. And, if you put faith in telling the truth regardless of how hard it may be, at least your girl will know she can trust you, no matter how badly you screw up.

Never 'multi-date'. Just like trying to watch two different movies on two screens simultaneously will dilute the experience of both, it's impossible to develop a meaningful connection with any woman if you're busy courting another. Spend a week or two getting to know each woman you like. If it doesn't seem to you that things could get serious with one woman, explain it clearly and gently, and move on.

Being good at dating and keeping your girlfriend's attention is easy. The hard part comes in working through a relationship's ups and downs through the years and taking it to its eventual conclusion. Of course, it's a lot less difficult if you're with the right person.

Finally, I'd like to thank you for reading this book! If you enjoyed it or found it helpful, I'd greatly appreciate it if you'd take a moment to leave a review on Amazon. Thank you!